The Wilderness
That Bears Your Name

The Wilderness
That Bears Your Name

poems

James A. Pearson

Goat Trail Press

Published by Goat Trail Press

ISBN 979-8-9902210-0-0

Book & cover design by James A. Pearson

For Elizabeth, whose wilderness invites me deeper into my own.

Contents

MUD SEASON

SPRING

SUMMER

Preface

*Walker, only your footprints
are the path, and nothing else;
Walker, there is no path...*
　　　　　　　–Antonio Machado

Today started off gray and drizzly here in the Pacific Northwest and showed no signs of changing.

There was nothing on the calendar. I made breakfast for my wife, Elizabeth. I did the laundry. I went for a walk in the woods and picked up some groceries for dinner. Just a slow winter Sunday a couple weeks after Imbolc, the cross-quarter day whose name translates to "in the belly."

It was the kind of day that can feel calm and luxurious, or it can be filled with a constant background anxiety that keeps poking at you and saying, "Shouldn't you be doing more?"

In this same season ten years ago all my days were like that: Wide open. Uncertain. Desperate.

The life I'd spent my twenties building had just crumbled. I had no money, no place to live, and no sense of what could be next. Some good friends offered to let me crash in their spare room out in the Oklahoma countryside while I sorted through a few years worth of burnout and tried to piece together some kind of way forward. I gratefully accepted.

I got there just in time to watch an unusually late fall descend into winter. Leaves shriveled and fell. Icicles grew in a little ravine near the house. One night the dogs' paw prints out front froze hard into the mud and became permanent fixtures for a while.

I grew up in Southern California and lived a lot of my twenties in equatorial East Africa. In many ways this was my first real winter.

I spent the short, cold days walking the property, cutting firewood, and trying all sorts of journaling practices and meditations and job searches in hopes that something would strike the flint of my heart and make a spark.

But nothing seemed to. Even the things I'd always loved, or thought I loved.

We heated the log-cabin-style house with firewood cut from dead trees on the property. I remember how after their leaves had fallen it was beyond my skill to tell if trees were dead or alive. I'd forgive them if they thought the same of me.

Imbolc is one of the great transitional moments of the year. The three months leading up to it are the darkest of the annual cycle, with the winter solstice smack in their center. The nights stretch out to their full length and settle in.

But come the beginning of February the light is finally making a comeback. One way to understand Imbolc is that it marks the transition from the season of steady night to a season of rapidly growing days. Everything starts to accelerate towards spring.

That's what I thought would happen coming out of that long Oklahoma winter. I thought my life would find it's momentum again. That it would carry me into a waiting spring.

But that's not how it went.

With the help of a kind mentor I found enough clarity to take my first few, crucial steps. I moved to Seattle to be closer to Elizabeth, back when I was first falling in love with her. I found a job that would help me get my financial footing. And I started to notice the first, subtle inklings that something might be alive and wanting to grow in me.

But this wasn't the rush of spring. This was some sort of murky, pathless middle ground. Years later I heard that in the northeastern U.S. they talk about a fifth season that comes between winter and spring. They call it the "mud season."

That's the season I was in.

Throughout that mud season one question kept circling its way back into my mind: "What is it that I really love in the world?"

I grew up knowing what I was supposed to love, what my family and my church and my country would reward me for loving. But this question was asking something different. It was asking what I love without all that. What do I love without reason or justification, just because I'm me, born into this world with my particular quirks and sensitivities?

When I first asked this question in the middle of my long winter I was terrified to admit that the honest answer was, "I don't really know." I felt a cold wash of shame that somehow I'd made it all the way into my thirties without answering such a basic question.

But as I trudged through the mud season I slowly learned to hold this question with less self-judgement and more curiosity. And when I gave it this kind of attention I noticed tiny stirrings inside me. They were nameless, barely perceptible. But they were there. Like buried seeds slowly waking after a long freeze.

That set me on a meandering path of exploration. As I followed those inklings into new ideas and experiences, I started to see a little constellation taking shape—a few points of curiosity and joy that formed the rough outline of an image I could move towards.

Poetry was one point in my constellation. And exploring my kinship with the natural world. Soul-level conversations were there, too, along with healthy, natural physical movement.

When Elizabeth and I were planning our wedding for the summer of 2019, I wanted to honor this emerging shape of myself by writing some poetry for the ceremony. So I started walking to the local coffee shop every morning and trying to do just that.

It took months. Some mornings I wouldn't find a single word to add to the lines that were slowly starting to emerge. But week by week a few poems took shape. One of them, "The Space Between Us," starts like this:

Don't try to give me
all of yourself—
as if you would,
as if the wilderness
that bears your name
was yours to give.

That idea of "the wilderness that bears your name" seeped into my consciousness. It's changed how I see myself, my wife, everyone I love and build relationships with.

In some ways this book is a chronicle of me slowly learning to embrace my own wilderness, through all its lawless seasons.

I wish I could tell you that I've finally settled into a warm and bountiful summer of life. But if I had to name the season I'm in right now, I'd say it's very early spring.

In spring the world does a million different experiments with life. The ones that survive become the fullness we see in summer. But many of them don't. Many of them start too early in the season, or come up in the wrong soil, or are crowded out by everything else that's trying to grow.

They say the name Imbolc is rooted in the way this happens with sheep in Ireland. As the days finally start growing noticeably longer, the next season's lambs are growing in the bellies of the ewes. Hence the Old Irish "i mbolc," or "in the belly."

As we crossed Imbloc a couple weeks ago I felt that meaning in a new way. Elizabeth is pregnant with our first child. A new and unknowable wilderness is about to bloom into our lives.

And my life feels pregnant, too. All these little loves I've been nurturing are slowly growing, knitting themselves together in ways I can't fully control or even imagine. If I *was* in control I'd ask them to knit together faster, to finally reveal my path into that abundant summer.

But that's not how a wilderness works.

If these poems are anything, they're invitations to be present to the full, wild, frustrating seasonality of a human life. To embrace more and more of that unreproducible wilderness that bears your name.

James A. Pearson
18th February, 2024

Prologue:
Vows to the Mystery

SOUTH

Turn with me to the south,
where the sun climbs
to the sky's peak,
flooding the world with
light and warmth, and inviting
the hidden sweetness in all things
to grow full and heavy
on the branches of the world.

You will know the summers of life,
when the sun and the shade,
the heat and the breeze,
the berries softening along the trail
all conspire for your satisfaction,
when the world's gifts overflow
the basket of your needs,
and your deep practice
is to rest in this abundance
with gratitude—giving freely
what has ripened in you.

WEST

Turn with me to the west,
where the sun falls
into the horizon's open arms
and the rising tide
of cold and dark
sends the shiver of change
through every living thing.

You will know the autumns of life,
when cherished pieces
of your world and yourself
wilt and wither,
when what has sustained you
is slipping away,
and only your faith—
that renewal
is the dancing partner of loss
—helps you trust
that the seeds of your
future wholeness
have already been planted.

NORTH

Turn with me to the north,
where silence fills
the dark globe of the night,
and the cold wind racing unchecked
through skeleton trees
sends all the plants and creatures
to seek shelter
in each other and the earth.

You will know the winters of life,
when dark nights of loss
stretch endlessly around you
and even the days are cold enough
to test the resilience
of your heart,
when the work of survival
takes all you have to give,
and you need the warmth
of each other's bodies
to make it through the night.

EAST

Turn with me to the east,
where the light grows like a promise
behind the mountains,
drawing up from the earth
the delicate hopes of new leaves,
new flowers opening,
new eyes alive to the world
for the first time.

You will know the springs of life,
when the hidden seeds
of your deep longing
finally push their first shoots
into the light of your days,
and your sacred responsibility
is to nurture this fragile growth,
even as it carves and shapes you
in frightening, wondrous ways.

VOWS

As these seasons of life come and go,
do you promise to meet them
with your whole heart,
as best you can?

The Wilderness
That Bears Your Name

Fall

The invitation of fall is to loosen your grip on the person you've needed to be, in order to make space for the person you're becoming.

ONE GOOD WIND

It's October so yes, the world
is dying but I always think
I have another month
at least, maybe two,
to marvel in the middle
of fall's kaleidoscope,
walking this fractal trance
of kindergarten yellows and
(somehow!) iridescent pinks.
But then one good wind
comes in off the distant Pacific
and trees that just yesterday
dripped with dazzle
stand skeletized, stripped
of their abundance
for the promiseless months to come.
I guess what I'm trying to say is:
Don't save up your praise.
Luxuriate fully in what you love
because the winds come quickly
and the winter is long.

THE SIMPLEST OF ALL REGRETS

I'm in one right now—
one of those days that will never
come again. The brown puzzle pieces
of oak leaves scattered
over the sidewalk, and the sunrise
stretching itself into a long,
luxurious thing. And you
sitting across from me laughing
to yourself about something
on your phone, totally unaware
of the alchemical morning light
against your cheek.
Please body! Please mind!
Wake fully into this moment!
How many days already
have I lost to that simplest
of all regrets: If only I had been
more present.

THE CRASH

The time for flying is over now,
but you knew that—
you're the one falling.

Yes, you are going to crash.
Yes, it will destroy you.
No, you will not be destroyed.

I know that doesn't make sense
and it never will, but someday
you'll say the same—

someday when your wreckage
has grown roots, and your
new wings help to lift us all.

WHEN THAT FIRE

The destroying fire
is coming into
the leaves
again—

oranges and deep
reds gathering
around the
edges,

preparing to consume
whole trees,
turn forests
into

boneyards. I remember
when that fire
came for
me.

THE WAY BACK

Sometimes you walk
away from yourself
for years, convinced
that what you're building
is your life,
unable anymore
to tell your own voice
from all the many voices
you've tried on,
unable to hear
your own voice
at all.

And you know now
the route back
will be terrible,
through every tender wasteland
you've been desperate
to avoid,
and with all
your many defenses
dropped
right here
in a pile where you stand,
where you finally turned around

and said,
"Enough."

No telling how long
this journey will take
or how much of you
it will cost.
But in this moment
some part of you knows
you have everything you need
to begin:
the compass arrow
of longing
tugging at your chest,
and the firm commitment
it's taken you all these years
to make—

that whatever the distance
you will take
every last step
back to where your soul
has kept the fire burning
and will never
let it die.

MORE THAN OKAY

I'm not wishing you failure,
or heartbreak, or the loss
of who you've worked so hard
to be. But I'm standing here
on the other side of my own
destruction, my bare feet
warming in the dark soil,
and I'm whispering little
ribbons into the wind that say,
"You're going to be more
than okay." You don't deserve
the pain of this world. But
no one arrives in their own life
without the cataclysm of birth.

THE TRAIL OF SEEDS

What started as flowers
are quickly becoming seeds,
brown and heavy on stalks
bent low to the earth.

I had a dream for my life.
It bloomed and withered
and left me laden with—
regrets, I thought, and fears.

For years the load I carried!
Until one day I found it
growing lighter on my shoulders,
and behind me a trail of seeds.

FEASTING SEASON

Come to the table
even if you're starving,
even if all you have to offer
is the weight
of what never grew.

Did you know a tree can break
under the burden
of its own fruit?

What you carry as shame
will be a feast
in the right mouth.
Your honest emptiness
drips with harvest.

WHERE DID THE MIDDLE GO?

It's always near the end
that I'm startled into presence—
my morning walk nearly over,
my coffee down to its last sip.
Where have I been? Where did
the middle go? I've been asking
all my life. But then what's ending
shakes me back into my body,
the way that fall calls to you
with its waving yellows and
falling reds: "Witness me!"
it seems to shout. "I'm here
only for a moment."

NOVEMBER EVENING

And then there's
the yellow trees dripping
with after-storm light.
And then the busy
people's faces, each
with its effortless beauty.
And then the steely, spacious
twilight glow in the west,
and to the east the tall poplar
shining dimly against
dark gray distant clouds.
And then I'm walking in
a world once again enchanted,
once again seducing me
back into wonder. And then,
just for a moment,
I remember who I am.

ABSOLUTELY NOTHING

What
did I ever do
in my life
to deserve
an apple
ripened on
this fledgling tree
under October
white-gray
with just the right amount
of wind?

Winter

The invitation of winter is to reconnect with the lost and wounded parts of yourself that hold the seeds of a new spring.

WINTERING

Now the leaves have fallen.
The trees have pulled their aliveness
back in from their branches,
down into their fortress trunks
and the dark, subterranean closeness
of their roots.

Every year they let go of
exactly what everyone says
is most beautiful about them
to save their own lives.

The time will come
when you, too, have to drop
all the ways you've made yourself
worth loving,
and finally learn how
to sit quietly
right in the center
of your own small life.

Only there can you cry the tears
your life depends on.
Only there will you find
the tiny seed
that holds the whole mystery of you

and cradle it
in the warmth of your body
until the spring.

AFTER SAMHAIN

Now, for a while, the dark
stays dark. The long nights
will be long no matter
how you pray for light.

This god will not be rushed.

But she will offer you
the thick black folds of her cloak,
where you're finally free
to lose everything
that can't be kept.

WINTER SOLSTICE

It happens in a moment—
this tiny, imperceptible turning
when all at once the night
ceases its imperial advance
and the next morning promises
to dawn just a sigh earlier
than the one before.

The world still goes on dying
around it, and trying to keep itself alive.
This is not yet the spring.

But huddled in their dens,
their nests, their thick forest groves,
the creatures of the world
put all their wordless faith in this
quiet shift, dreaming songs of hope
that maybe, even now,
it's already happened.

ALL I MEAN

There are a thousand
wounds but all I mean
by healing is this:

that you learn to hold yourself
in exactly the way
you were never held.

SURROUNDED

Look how this wilderness
swept in around us—
while we slept,
while we paid the rent,
while we ordered another round.

By the time we looked up
all our paths were gone.
The forest presses in on all sides,
every direction an equal mystery
of tangle and dark.

Breathe now.

Breathe down into
your wild body,
its sudden alertness,
its burning need to keep you safe.
There are parts of you that know
how to stand still in this place,
parts of you that will know
which step to take.

A NEW PRACTICE

To not be able to move
my body towards the scared,
the lonely, the grieving—
this is a new practice
in holding my heart open
longer than I know how.

WHAT NEEDS YOU

Sit still
and you will find
discomfort.

Sit still
in the discomfort
and you will find

what needs you.

THE DAY MARY OLIVER DIED

There are trees
in the forest near my home
that hold the world together,
their roots married
to the bones of the earth.

The little boy in me knows
they are eternal.
The man I've become
has seen them fallen,
their ancient trunks softening,
the borders between themselves and everything
opening, slowly opening.

If only she could tell us now
what it is to fall.
How would the sharp praise of her voice
shape that long, slow exhale
of becoming
what so astonished her?

ABSENCE

There's so much beauty
in the lives
I haven't lived,
like the blue
in these mountain shadows—
unreproducible
in any other world
but this one
where it only exists
as absence.

THE FIRST PROMISE

Sometimes you need to hide
from everything you've
promised to become,
so you can find the first promise:
the one you and the soft world
sang to each other

down beneath the tall bushes
along the old streambed,
back when nobody knew
exactly where you were,
before the person
everyone needed you to be
learned to find you even there.

That place is just a memory
but the sanctuary still waits—
in the quiet places under trees,
the spacious darkness
of a solitary night—
and if you learn again
how to hide, even from

the expectations you've
mistaken for your own,
you'll find the world still knows

your secret harmony,
and that some brave and
brokenhearted voice in you
never stopped singing.

HOW MANY THINGS

Look how many things
I've turned out

not to be—
what a bitter

gift.

THE HOLY MELANCHOLY

Come thou Holy Melancholy,
Wound my heart to weep thy grace.
Deepest well of precious longing,
Let your tears anoint my face.

Come meet me in the twilit evening,
Beneath the weight of descending night.
It's here your bitter does the sweet'ning,
Your dark the only home for light.

I tried to sing all songs of gladness,
Only happy notes employ,
But they rang hollow of your sadness,
Base note to the chords of joy.

Come burst dams of my defenses,
Your waters carving like a knife,
Lay bare my heart and tender senses,
To live a broken open life.

SELF-COMPASSION

Remember that a lake
can freeze
and unfreeze
a thousand times

and feel no shame.

THE HUMMINGBIRD

From the corner of my eye
a hummingbird
hovers and zigs
just outside
the little basement window
beside my desk.

But when
I turn to look,
it's only a brown leaf
suspended in a spiderweb
being trembled
by the wind.

All day long
it goes like this:
the hummingbird playing
at the edge of vision;
the dead leaf waiting
to meet my glance—

Trust me when I tell you
that some part of you knows
what you love.
Look how it flirts with you
hour after hour
at the threshold of your life.

STANDING INVITATION

Come home to
this body. It's living
your life.

Mud Season

The mud season is that uncertain time between winter and spring, when you're invited to hold close what's new and tender in you as you step out into the pathless world.

THE MUD SEASON

Patience darling,
it's still too early
to trust the season
with that tenderness you hold
in your globed hands.

I can feel it, too—
the yearning to plant
your fingers in the warming earth
and release what's so alive in you
into the scrum of all life.

But the ground's still frozen
beneath all this mud;
and winter, even on its way out,
will take with it anything
that opens too soon.

So hold your longing
a little longer
in the sheltered care of your body,
like soft green starts
on the windowsill of your heart,
seedlings from the tree
of good and evil.

WEATHER AND FLESH

Can you survive this cold April?
This second winter
when there should be sun?

Can you accept that you feel—
right now, in this moment
—exactly what you feel?

This body won't be bound by forecasts.
It's as inevitable as the sky,
as much weather as flesh.

TRADECRAFT

This is the season
for disappearing.
Slip away
to where no one knows
to find you.
Meet yourself
right where you've always hungered
to be met.

Now's the time to cheat
on all the names
you've taught the world to call you,
to be unfaithful
to who you thought you wanted
to become.

Plan a hundred
secret rendezvous
with the delicious stranger
you're discovering
yourself to be.

Don't tell a soul what you're doing
or where it is you go at all hours.
Be clandestine.
Protect the source.

PERMISSION TO LOSE INTEREST

Looking up through the windshield at
dark wings and a white head
crossing high above I-5. "Just a seagull,"

I hear myself say—permission
to lose interest, permission to shut down
the aqueducts of wonder. How quickly

I abandon my enchantment, like it's
a grenade about to bloom or a great eye
opening. Because really I know

that the shape of those wings
cutting against a blue sky
is a beauty sharp enough to cut me, too.

HOW TO LISTEN

I'm not asking you
to come down here
and clean out the muddy
corners of my life.

I'm asking you
to be a forest
where mud and leaves,
shadows and light,
growth and decay
all have their unquestioned
belonging.

I'm asking you
to be an ocean
where even great storms
don't trouble the depths
and each tear is welcomed
as a homecoming.

I'm asking you
to be as spacious
as the vast darkness
behind the sky,
which will never be afraid
of what I do
or don't choose.

I'm not asking you
to hold me together.
I'm asking you
to open so wide
there's room for all the ways
I come apart.

WHAT TO DO AFTER VOTING

Take back that part of yourself
you lent to politicians.
Peel their slogans from your mouth
and pledge your allegiance
to the mother down the street
whose kids have grown out of
their summer shoes again.

And if you're going to raise a flag
let it be the flag of forgiveness,
the flag of our complicity
in so much we say we're against.
Under that flag you and I
can plant a small new world
and nurture it as it grows.

NEW GLASSES

I just got new glasses
so my eyes are re-learning
the length of my body,
how to guide my feet
from rock to rock.
Even after all these years
the different parts of me
are still working things out.
How can I ever hope to know
you? All the way over there
in a body of your own.

THE GIFT YOU SEEK

You spend your whole life
looking for something,
only to find

the world looking back at you,
saying, "Yes, please give us
this gift you seek."

JET-LAGGED IN CHANIA

Sunrise light falls down
the hotels and tavernas
along the old port,
brightening the colorful facades.
What kind of light would reveal
all the glory those facades
were built to hide?

Each one is crumbling
in its own secret way.
Inside each one is a family
hiding the knives of their uncertainty
from each other.

All the million photos
of this lovely little port
can't match the transcendence
of a gray-stubbled man
wiping down the plastic chairs
outside his cafe, resigning himself
to another day in paradise.

He knows the truth
it's taken me all these years to learn:
that there's nothing pretty enough
to be beautiful.

CANDLE SMOKE

This candle smoke
that's white
against the shaded room
is dark against the window light.

Maybe we're neither
good nor bad.

Maybe we're smoke rising
from tiny embers of
life, almost gone,
making beautiful shapes.

STEALING GOD'S POWER

If at the end
of all your praying
God finally speaks to you
and lists the many ways
you need to change
another person,

that's not God.

That's a child
playing dress-up
in a white beard,
stealing God's power,
terrified to discover
that love
and control
annihilate each other.

GAME TRAILS

The forest closes behind me
and now this subtle path at my feet
is the red thread between worlds,
a path made by the soft steps
of wild things, who are at home
in the tangled mystery.

But I am new to this way of walking—
how the trail flirts and teases,
fading and hiding and calling you on;
how it disappears and makes you choose
before revealing itself again;
how it tempts you with
countless branching connections
so you could end up anywhere
you didn't want to be.

But if you move slowly, softly,
pausing to fully arrive
at each new revelation,
you can find—among a thousand paths
through the forest—the one path
that knows your name.

Spring

The invitation of spring is to risk bringing what's new and tender in you out into the unruly world.

NOBODY KNEW

Nobody knew
the cherry trees
would bloom today.
How quietly

they must have
whispered together,
huddled in the
deepest ends

of their roots,
as winter's death crept
down their branches.
But slowly—

as slowly as the Earth
tilts her head
back towards the sun
—a chorus grew,

some ancient hymn
of faith, and the life
they'd been protecting
took heart and began

to rise into
scarred trunks
and broken branches
until all at once,

all over this gray city,
a million newborn
flowers proclaimed
the spring.

ALL THAT'S REQUIRED OF YOU

Did you know
there will be poppies
again this year?
It's true. I've seen
their muted green fractals
stockpiling sunlight,
distilling it down
to its purest essence
before igniting
into slow motion fireworks.

In the end, isn't this all
that's required of you?

To drink in what you love,
to concentrate it
in the crucible of your body,
and, finally, to bloom.

MEANWHILE

Meanwhile the world's still doing spring
like nothing's happening. There was sunlight
on the forest floor today, and the sounds of birds

welcoming themselves home to another place
they still belong. My fears found no corroboration
in the old growth Douglas firs, who seemed

as steady as ever. Not even the swarms
of little hemlocks clawing towards the light
echoed my alarm. They all just let me be there

with all the hornets buzzing in my chest.
Some mirrors are big enough to show you
how even the end of the world really isn't.

WHAT SPRING DOES

Some winters
are so long
you can forget
what spring does

until it does it.

THE SOUTHERN COAST OF CRETE

Looking south over the Mediterranean,
past Gavdos, into the space
between Europe and Africa,
where two great and ancient gods
breathe back and forth, asking
their painful questions of each other.

So much to forgive
in these troubled centuries. Even now,
a new heartbreak every moment.
But still at their depths they hold together,
their locked arms cradling
the blue jewel of the sea.

Look how gently these little waves,
sent from such a distance,
caress the rocky shore.
Tell me that's not how lovers touch.

A NEW SPRING

Today for the first time in months
the sun was strong enough
for me to sit outside in the afternoon,
sipping a cold drink, my body remembering
a season when the world wanted me

to be alive, to grow. But that was before
all the dying I've done—whole futures fallen,
promises left hanging like fishhooks.
Would spring come again, even for me?
And if it did would it find me brave enough
to risk a new seed in the trickster soil?

Who knows what shapes this life might take?!
But this I do know: the only regret
is not loving the world
in all the painfully honest ways
that only you can love it.

IMAGINE

You are not
this runted little tree
shiver-dancing near the top
of an overlooked mountain,
fated to the thin, rocky
soil of your life.

But imagine if you were.

Imagine if
all you had to do
to be beautiful
was to let the wind
dance you where you stand
as you grow into
the only shape
you ever had.

THIS SPRING

How can I love this spring
when it's pulling me
through my life faster
than any time before it?
When five separate dooms
are promised this decade
and here I am, just trying
to watch a bumblebee cling
to its first purple flower.
I cannot save this world.
But look how it's trying,
once again, to save me.

SPRING'S INVITATION

The cherry blossoms
are already falling
in small drifts
of pink snow.
The dogwood petals
are showing their age.
Each year spring
gives her whole self
to test the openness
of your heart—
"Will you join me?"
the invitation echoes
through the warming air.
"Will you give your life?"

HOW TO BUILD A TREE

Sometimes your next
halting step
is more powerful
than the grandest vision.

All a leaf knows
about building a tree
is to turn towards the light.

Summer

The invitation of summer is to give and receive wholeheartedly, immersed in the full flow of your belonging in the world.

WORKER BEES

I wonder if you can pause
—just for a moment—
the emergency of your life
and step out into
the quiet of the world.

Hear how gently it conveys
the delicate thread of birdsong,
how quickly it can soothe
the rupture of a passing jet.
Feel its vast, smiling invitation
to rest back into the person
you've been all your life.

Listen now–
the poppies bursting
out over the sidewalk
are electric with bees.
Look how they bury their bodies
in flower after flower, drunk
on their longing for the world.

Maybe that's the real work:
to fall, over and over,
into the scent of what you love.

A SIMPLE OFFERING

Just before noon I step out back
to take a break from wondering
what my life will become.
The sun is on the flower bed,
turning the poppies into
small bowls of light.

How simply they make
their offering:
nectar for the bees,
pollen for each other,
subtle bows to their low sky.

One flower is just emerging
from its small green cocoon,
the rich orange petals still sheathed
in the home it's grown out of.
I kneel down and—
like the gentlest prayer
—slide off its whole, close world.

I guess sometimes birth comes easy.
Sometimes it's as simple as revealing
what's already whole.

IT'S IN EVERYTHING

It's in everything, this dancing
of something that's more than just life.
Look at the trees near the shore,
how they shimmy and wave
over the bright face of the Salish Sea.

Meanwhile the waters rush in,
mad for the moon, twirling around
the outstretched hand of the point
and kissing the forehead of the beach
before they rush back out again.

I have it on good authority
that the whole world spins and spins
as it falls toward the warm center of its love,
then swings back out
to sing of it among the stars.

Stand still here among the trees
and the wind and the warm sun.
What dance stirs in the bones of you to join?
Let the music of the world find you.

WHAT I'M TRYING TO SAY

I'm not saying it's been easy,
this life. Harder, in fact,
than you ever expected.
What I'm saying is that
every one of your mornings
has been met by the sun rising.
Every time you made a dollar
it was met by an apple,
whose firm white flesh—
a partnership of tree and rain,
of sunlight and farmer and soil
—is no different than a miracle.
What I'm trying to say is
the world has worked wonders
to make sure there's been ground
beneath every one of your steps.
You were never alone.
Even now you can lean back
into the strong arms of this moment
and let yourself be held
by what's always held you.
Every day there's a reason
to bathe your life in gratitude.

THE SPACE BETWEEN US

Don't try to give me
all of yourself—
as if you would,
as if the wilderness
that bears your name
was yours to give.

Instead let's live
like mountains: two worlds
rooted together but each
cutting our own shape
into the changing sky.

I'll be the one to see you
radiant in the morning light,
and to watch as evening's last glow
anoints your head.

I'll be your companion
as the seasons paint you
green and gold and white
and green again.

And as the snows melt
and the rains fall,
carving ever deeper

the beautiful grooves of your being,
let them flow down into

the sacred space between us—
this quiet valley our bodies make,
where deep waters
and the dark earth

take everything we've lost
and everything we've given
and make new life
for all who call this place
home.

LEAVING CRETE

It's still night-dark
when we drive out of Rethymno.
The headlights on our little blue rental
show us nothing
of the stone-spined island
we're already leaving.
It took us six years to get here.

Though neither of us knew—back when
our glances for each other were filled
with the first tender questions—
where here would be.
Or that a whole love story
would live in the soft glow
of our shared memory.

For fourteen sun-blessed days
here on the island where Ariadne
showed Theseus the secret of the labyrinth
we've laid down our own red thread,
tracing moments we'll whisper to each other
for the rest of our lives—
a hidden cove, doors left open to the sea,
a canyon through the mountains
carved just for us.

Now our promises reel us back
towards dark skies and shortening days.
Be as we wind along this jagged coast
one last time, the sky lightens
just enough to outline
the black mystery of the hills,
as signs for places still unknown to us
flash through the headlights—Kirianna,
Damasta, Roumeli—invitations
to what we have not yet imagined.

YOU TAKE IT WITH YOU

Remember
that you take it with you.
All of it. Even the fuzzy
and forgotten parts.

It's all there
in the way you breathe now,
in the questions you never
would have thought to ask,

in the new sense
by which you navigate
the world outside,
and the world within.

The legacy of every moment
beats within you—
fifty, eighty,
one hundred times a minute.

SEPTEMBER NOW

September now
and the summer sighs along.
Only those who know it
catch its meaning.

As I grow old may I lengthen
like these late summer shadows,
every day embracing
a little more of
this needless world.

THIS IS NOT THE END

This is not
the end.
News that may come
as a salve
in the dry cold of winter,
or like an unwelcome tug
on the hammock
of August.
However finished
you're afraid you are
or wish
you could be,
remember:

this earth that rests
so still beneath you
is racing around the sun,
teaching your body
to dance the seasons.
You are carried
with a million years
of faith: that there is more in you
longing to break open,
to pour out,
to mingle
with the soil of life.

Acknowledgements

There's no way to list or even to remember all the ways people have nudged and supported me towards this book. But it wouldn't exist without them. So I want to at least try to express some of the gratitude I feel.

First to my wife, Elizabeth Moreno, whose buoyant and undemanding belief in me helped create the space for this book to grow, and whose insights and feedback made it better.

To my mom, who has championed my writing since I was a boy, and to my dad for his steady optimism and encouragement. To my sisters, Jessica Connolly and Robin Fox, who have become two of my best friends in adulthood, and who I can always count on for groundedness and support.

To my friends Aaron, Christen, and Xavier Campbell, who put me up—and put up with me— during my long winter. And to my friend Glenn Parrish, who mentored me through it.

To my friend Andy Lang, who went first on this publishing adventure and has been unfailingly generous with his experience.

To my friend Graham Murtaugh, whose poetic conversations and camaraderie expanded the scope of my writing and sharpened my voice.

To all my friends who've encouraged and complimented my writing—I don't know that I would have kept going without you. I'm a product of the people who've cheered me on.

To all the folks who've shared stories with me about how my poems connected with their lives—you helped me trust that my work has power in the world.

To every person who's asked me when they could get a book of my poetry—you helped me imagine this book might actually find a home in the world.

To everyone who's subscribed to my email list, follows me on social media, shares, likes, and comments on my work—you're why I thought this book might be possible in the first place.

And if you're reading this, I'm grateful to you for giving this book and these poems a place to land. I always feel that once you put a poem out into the world, it needs to find someone's heart to live in. I hope one or two of mine might find a home with you.

More from James A. Pearson

I regularly send out new poems, articles, and invitations to people who subscribe to my email list. To get my latest work just open your camera app and scan this QR code:

or go to:

jamesapearson.com/wilderness

When you sign up you'll get a free workbook I made to go along with this book.

It's designed to help you gather the deepest gifts this season of life has to offer you. I hope it serves you well.

Printed in Great Britain
by Amazon